A PLAN
for
IMPROVING FEMALE EDUCATION
By Emma Willard

and

MRS. EMMA WILLARD'S
LIFE AND WORK IN MIDDLEBURY

By Ezra Brainerd, L.L.D.
President of Middlebury College, 1885-1908

LARLIN CORPORATION
Marietta, Georgia
1987

Library of Congress Cataloging-in-Publication Data

Willard, Emma, 1787-1870.
  A plan for improving female education.

  Reprint (1st work). Originally published: Middlebury, Vt. : Middlebury College, 1918.
  Reprint (2nd work). Originally published: Middlebury, Vt. : Middlebury College, 1918.
  Includes index.
  1. Higher education of women--United States--History.
  2. Women--Education--United States--History. 3. Educational equalization--United States--History. 4. Sex discrimination in education--United States--History.
  5. Willard, Emma, 1787-1870. I. Brainerd, Ezra, 1844-1924. Mrs. Emma Willard's life and work in Middlebury. 1987. II. Title.

LC1756.W65   1987   376'.973   87-32477
ISBN 0-89783-044-X (pbk. : alk. paper)

A Plan for Improving Female Education was originally published in 1818 in Middlebury, Vermont.   This is a reprint of the Second Edition, offset from an edition published by Middlebury College in 1918 on the 100th anniversary of the issue of the first edition.

Mrs. Emma Willard's Life and Work in Middlebury was originally delivered as a speech in 1888 or 1889 to the Emma Willard Society at the home of Mrs. Russell Sage in New York City. The remarks were later included in the United States Bureau of Education Circular of Information No. 4, 1900, Whole Number 265, Vol. No. 29 **History of Education in Vermont,** pages 130-137.

This book is printed on acid-free paper which conforms to the American National Standard Z39.48-1984 *Permanence of Paper for Printed Library Materials.* Paper that conforms to this standard's requirements for pH, alkaline reserve and freedom from groundwood is anticipated to last several hundred years without significant deterioration under normal library use and storage conditions. ∞

Manufactured in the United States of America
ISBN: 0-89783-044-X
97 96 95 94 93 92 91 90 89 88 87   10 9 8 7 6 5 4 3 2 1

  Larlin Corporation
P.O. Box 1523, Marietta, GA 30061

Cover design by Paulette Lambert.

The following pages reproduce without change a document which has been called the Magna Carta of the higher education of women in America. It was written during the two or three years preceding 1819 in Middlebury, in a house just across the street from the campus of Middlebury College. Some years earlier Mrs. Willard had conducted in Middlebury a school for young women not essentially different from the boarding schools she condemns so vigorously. It was in contact with the worthier education offered to young men in the college that she developed her conviction of the need of radical change in the education of women and the principles she put in force in her second school in Middlebury, which was later removed to Troy.

The world war and its attendant changes in the position and occupations of women is leading to a re-examination of the purposes and methods of women's education. This notable address of one of the great pioneers in the higher education of women in America is re-published, not merely as a bit of antiquarian zeal on the part of the college which furnished stimulus and suggestion to its author, but also as a statement of principles and ideals which ought not to be neglected in the effort to adapt the higher education of women to the larger place in the life of the world which they are henceforth to occupy.

Introduction to the edition published by
Middlebury College in 1918

Explanatory Note

Timely interest in the enclosed pamphlet written by Emma Willard, pioneer in the education of women at Middlebury, Vermont, over 100 years ago, is given by the fact that Mrs. Russell Sage, who was a great admirer of the work of Mrs. Willard, has just left to Middlebury College the sum of $100,000.

The Middlebury Register in its issue of November 22, 1918, contains the following interesting statement by Dr. Ezra Brainerd, president-emeritus of the College, indicating how Mrs. Sage became interested in Middlebury:

"About thirty years ago I received an invitation to give a talk on the life and work of Emma Willard during the twelve years she lived in Middlebury when from 20 to 32 years of age. This talk was to be given before the Emma Willard Association in New York City, at the home on Fifth Avenue of Mrs. Russell Sage, who was the President of the Association. I met there an interesting company who held in high esteem the mature matron under whose guidance they had graduated from the famous Ladies Seminary in Troy. It was not difficult to interest them in an account of Emma Willard's early life and of her confessed indebtedness to Middlebury College for her advanced views regarding the higher education of women. I succeeded in securing $2000 for an Emma Willard scholarship in Middlebury College. The following year came an invitation to address them again, and to publish a pamphlet containing the substance of my talks. This was done at the expense of a New York lawyer, a former pupil of mine, whose mother in Vermont was a graduate of the Troy Seminary. The pamphlet passed through two editions of 500 copies each, most of which were placed in the hands of Mrs. Sage for distribution to the graduates of the Troy Seminary.

"This pamphlet was later republished by the United States Bureau of Education, Circular of Information No. 4, 1900; whole number 265. On page 130, under the headline of the article, the reader is informed that it was 'prepared originally for the Emma Willard Society of New York by Ezra Brainerd, LL. D., President of Middlebury College.'

"Thus it would appear probable that the 100,000 dollar bequest is the fair fruitage of the humble seed sown in faith so many years ago."

From the edition published by
Middlebury College in 1918.

AN ADDRESS

TO THE PUBLIC;

PARTICULARLY

TO THE MEMBERS OF THE

LEGISLATURE

OF

NEW-YORK,

PROPOSING

A PLAN

FOR IMPROVING

FEMALE EDUCATION,

BY EMMA WILLARD.

SECOND EDITION.

MIDDLEBURY:
PRINTED BY J. W. COPELAND,
1819.

ADDRESS, &C.

HE object of this Address, is to convince the public, that a reform, with respect to female education, is necessary; that it cannot be effected by individual exertion, but that it requires the aid of the legislature; and further, by shewing the justice, the policy, and the magnanimity of such an undertaking, to persuade that body to endow a seminary for females, as the commencement of such reformation.

The idea of a college for males will naturally be associated with that of a seminary, instituted and endowed by the public; and the absurdity of sending ladies to college, may, at first thought, strike every one to whom this subject shall be proposed. I therefore hasten to observe, that the seminary here recommended, will be as different from those appropriated to the other sex, as the female character and duties are from the male. The business of the husbandman is not to waste his endeavours, in seeking to make his orchard attain the strength and majesty of his forest, but to rear each, to the perfection of its nature.

That the improvement of female education will be considered by our enlightened citizens as a subject of importance, the liberality with which they part with their property to educate their daughters, is a sufficient evidence; and why should they not, when assembled in the legislature, act in concert to effect a noble object, which, though dear to them individually, cannot be accomplished by their unconnected exertions.

If the improvement of the American female character, and that alone, could be effected by public liberality, employed in giving better means of instruction;

such improvement of one half of society, and that half, which barbarous and despotic nations have ever degraded, would of itself be an object, worthy of the most liberal government on earth; but if the female character be raised, it must inevitably raise that of the other sex: and thus does the plan proposed, offer, as the object of legislative bounty, to elevate the whole character of the community.

As evidence that this statement does not exaggerate the female influence in society, our sex need but be considered, in the single relation of mothers. In this character, we have the charge of the whole mass of individuals, who are to compose the succeeding generation; during that period of youth, when the pliant mind takes any direction, to which it is steadily guided by a forming hand. How important a power is given by this charge! yet, little do too many of my sex know how, either to appreciate or improve it. Unprovided with the means of acquiring that knowledge, which flows liberally to the other sex—having our time of education devoted to frivolous acquirements, how should we understand the nature of the mind, so as to be aware of the importance of those early impressions, which we make upon the minds of our children?—or how should we be able to form enlarged and correct views, either of the character, to which we ought to mould them, or of the means most proper to form them aright?

Considered in this point of view, were the interests of male education alone to be consulted, that of females becomes of sufficient importance to engage the public attention. Would we rear the human plant to its perfection, we must first fertilize the soil which produces it. If it acquire its first bent and texture upon a barren plain, it will avail comparatively little, should it be afterwards transplanted to a garden.

In the arrangement of my remarks, I shall pursue the following order.
I. Treat of the defects of the present mode of female education, and their causes.
II. Consider the principles, by which education should be regulated.
III. Sketch a plan of a female seminary.
IV. Shew the benefits which society would receive from such seminaries.

DEFECTS IN THE PRESENT MODE OF FEMALE EDUCATION, AND THEIR CAUSES.

Civilized nations have long since been convinced that education, as it respects males, will not, like trade, regulate itself; and hence, they have made it a prime object to provide that sex with everything requisite to facilitate their progress in learning: but female education has been left to the mercy of private adventurers; and the consequence has been to our sex, the same, as it would have been to the other, had legislatures left their accommodations, and means of instruction, to chance also.

Education cannot prosper in any community, unless, from the ordinary motives which actuate the human mind, the best and most cultivated talents of that community, can be brought into exercise in that way. Male education flourishes, because, from the guardian care of legislatures, the presidencies and professorships of our colleges are some of the highest objects to which the eye of ambition is directed. Not so with female institutions. Preceptresses of these, are dependent on their pupils for support, and are consequently liable to become the victims of their caprice. In such a situation, it is not more desirable to be a preceptress, than it would be, to be a parent, invested with the care of children, and responsible for their behaviour, but yet, depending on them for subsistence, and destitute of power to enforce their obedience.

Feminine delicacy requires, that girls should be educated chiefly by their own sex. This is apparent from considerations, that regard their health and conveniences, the propriety of their dress and manners, and their domestic accomplishments.

Boarding schools, therefore, whatever may be their defects, furnish the best mode of education provided for females.

Concerning these schools it may be observed:

1. They are temporary institutions, formed by individuals, whose object is present emolument. But they cannot be expected to be greatly lucrative; therefore, the individuals who establish them, cannot afford to provide suitable accommodations, as to room. At night, the pupils are frequently crowded in their lodging rooms; and during the day they are generally placed together in one apartment, where there is a heterogeneous mixture of different kinds of business, accompanied with so much noise and confusion, as greatly to impede their progress in study.

2. As individuals cannot afford to provide suitable accommodations as to room, so neither can they afford libraries, and other apparatus, necessary to teach properly the various branches in which they pretend to instruct.

3. Neither can the individuals who establish these schools afford to provide suitable instruction. It not unfrequently happens, that one instructress teaches, at the same time and in the same room, ten or twelve distinct branches. If assistants are provided, such are

usually taken as can be procured for a small compensation. True, in our large cities, preceptresses provide their pupils with masters, though at an expense, which few can afford. Yet none of these masters are responsible for the general proficiency or demeanour of the pupils. Their only responsibility, is in the particular branch which they teach; and to a preceptress, who probably does not understand it herself, and who is, therefore incapable of judging, whether or not it is well taught.

4. It is impossible, that in these schools such systems should be adopted and enforced, as are requisite for properly classing the pupils. Institutions for young gentlemen are founded by public authority, and are permanent; they are endowed with funds, and their instructors and overseers, are invested with authority to make such laws, as they shall deem most salutary. From their permanency, their laws and rules are well known. With their funds they procure libraries, philosophical apparatus, and other advantages, superior to what can elsewhere be found; and to enjoy these, individuals are placed under their discipline, who would not else be subjected to it. Hence the directors of these institutions can enforce, among other regulations, those which enable them to make a perfect classification of their students. They regulate their qualifications for entrance, the kind and order of their studies, and the period of their remaining at the seminary. Female schools present the reverse of this. Wanting permanency, and dependent on individual patronage, had they the wisdom to make salutary regulations, they could neither enforce nor purchase compliance. The pupils are irregular in their times of entering and leaving school; and they are of various and dissimilar acquirements.

Each scholar, of mature age, thinks she has a right to judge for herself respecting what she is to be taught; and the parents of those, who are not, consider, that they have the same right to judge for them. Under such disadvantages, a school cannot be classed, except in a very imperfect manner.

5. It is for the interest of instructresses of boarding schools, to teach their pupils showy accomplishments, rather than those, which are solid and useful. Their object in teaching is generally present profit. In order to realize this, they must contrive to give immediate celebrity to their schools. If they attend chiefly to the cultivation of the mind, their work may not be manifest at the first glance; but let the pupil return home, laden with fashionable toys, and her young companions, filled with envy and astonishment, are never satisfied till they are permitted to share the precious instruction. If it is true, with the turn of the fashion, the toys, which they are taught to make will become obsolete; and no benefit remain to them, of perhaps the only money, that will ever be expended on their education; but the object of the instructress may be accomplished notwithstanding, if that is directed to her own, rather than her pupil's advantage.

6. As these schools are private establishments, their preceptresses are not accountable to any particular persons. Any woman has a right to open a school in any place; and no one, either from law or custom, can prevent her. Hence the public are liable to be imposed upon, both with respect to the character and acquirements of preceptresses. I am far, however, from asserting that this is always the case. It has been before observed, that in the present state of things, the ordinary motives which actuate the human mind, would not induce ladies of the best and most cultivated tal-

ents, to engage in the business of instructing, from choice. But some have done it from necessity, and occasionally, an extraordinary female has occupied herself in instructing, because she felt that impulse to be active and useful, which is the characteristic of a vigorous and noble mind; and because she found few avenues to extensive usefulness open to her sex. But if such has been the fact, it has not been the consequence of any system, from which a similar result can be expected to recur with regularity; and it remains true, that the public are liable to imposition, both with regard to the character and acquirements of preceptresses.

Instances have lately occurred, in which women of bad reputation, at a distance from scenes of their former life, have been entrusted by our unsuspecting citizens with the instruction of their daughters.

But the moral reputation of individuals, is more a matter of public notoriety than their literary attainments; hence society are more liable to be deceived with regard to the acquirements of instructresses than with respect to their characters.

Those women, however, who deceive society as to the advantages which they give their pupils, are not charged with any ill intention. They teach as they were taught, and believe that the public are benefitted by their labours. Acquiring, in their youth, a high value for their own superficial accomplishments, they regard all others as supernumerary, if not unbecoming. Although these considerations exculpate individuals, yet they do not diminish the injury which society receives; for they show, that the worst which is to be expected from such instruction, is not that the pupils will remain ignorant; but that, by adopting the views of their teachers, they will have their minds barred against future improvement, by acquiring a disrelish, if not a contempt for useful knowledge.

7. Although, from a want of public support, preceptresses of boarding schools have not the means of enforcing such a system as would lead to a perfect classification of their pupils; and although they are confined in other respects within narrow limits, yet, because these establishments are not dependant on any public body, within those limits, they have a power far more arbitrary and uncontrolled, than is allowed the learned and judicious instructors of our male seminaries.

They can, at their option, omit their own duties, and excuse their pupils from theirs.

They can make absurd and ridiculous regulations.

They can make improper and even wicked exactions of their pupils.

Thus the writer has endeavoured to point out the defects of the present mode of female education; chiefly in order to show, that the great cause of these defects consists in a state of things, in which legislatures, undervaluing the importance of women in society, neglect to provide for their education, and suffer it to become the sport of adventurers for fortune, who may be both ignorant and vicious.

OF THE PRINCIPLES BY WHICH EDUCATION SHOULD BE REGULATED.

To contemplate the principles which should regulate systems of instruction, and consider how little those principles have been regarded in educating our sex, will show the defects of female education in a still stronger point of light, and will also afford a standard, by which any plan for its improvement may be measured.

Education should seek to bring its subjects to the perfection of their moral, intellectual and physical nature: in order, that they may be of the greatest possible use to themselves and others: or, to use a different expression, that they may be the means of the greatest possible happiness of which they are capable, both as to what they enjoy, and what they communicate.

Those youth have the surest chance of enjoying and communicating happiness, who are best qualified, both by internal dispositions, and external habits, to perform with readiness, those duties, which their future life will most probably give them occasion to practice.

Studies and employments should, therefore, be selected, from one or both of the following considerations; either, because they are peculiarly fitted to improve the faculties; or, because they are such, as the pupil will most probably have occasion to practise in future life.

These are the principles, on which systems of male education are founded; but female education has not yet been systematized. Chance and confusion reign here. Not even is youth considered in our sex, as in the other, a season, which should be wholly devoted to improvement. Among families, so rich as to be entirely above labour, the daughters are hurried through the routine of boarding school instruction, and at an early period introduced into the gay world; and, thenceforth, their only object is amusement.—Mark the different treatment, which the sons of these families receive. While their sisters are gliding through the mazes of the midnight dance, they employ the lamp, to treasure up for future use the riches of ancient wisdom; or to gather strength and expansion of mind, in exploring the wonderful paths of philosophy. When the youth of two sexes has been spent so differently, is it strange, or is nature in fault, if more mature age has brought such a difference of character, that our sex have been considered by the other, as the pampered, wayward babies of society, who must have some rattle put into our hands, to keep us from doing mischief to ourselves or others?*

Another difference in the treatment of the sexes is made in our country, which, though not equally pernicious to society, is more pathetically unjust to our sex. How often have we seen a student, who, returning from his literary pursuits, finds a sister, who was his equal in acquirements, while their advantages were equal, of whom he is now ashamed. While his youth was devoted to study, and he was furnished with the means, she, without any object of improvement, drudged at home, to assist in the support of the father's family, and perhaps to contribute to her brother's subsistence abroad; and now, a being of a lower order, the rustic innocent wonders and weeps at his neglect.

Not only has there been a want of system concerning female education, but much of what has been done, has proceeded upon mistaken principles.

One of these is, that, without a regard to the different periods of life, proportionate to their importance, the education of females has been too exclusively directed, to fit them for displaying to advantage the charms of youth and beauty. Though it may be proper to adorn this period of life, yet, it is incomparably more important, to prepare for the serious duties of maturer years. Though well to decorate the blossom, it is far better to prepare for the harvest. In the vegetable creation, nature seems but to sport, when she embellishes

---

*Several noted writers have recommended certain accomplishments to our sex, to keep us from scandal and other vices; or to use Mr. Addison's expression, "to keep us out of harm's way."

the flower; while all her serious cares are directed to perfect the fruit.

Another errour is, that it has been made the first object in educating our sex, to prepare them to please the other. But reason and religion teach, that we too are primary existencies; that it is for us to move, in the orbit of our duty, around the Holy Centre of perfection, the companions, not the satellites of men; else, instead of shedding around us an influence, that may help to keep them in their proper course, we must accompany them in their wildest deviations.

I would not be understood to insinuate, that we are not, in particular situations, to yield obedience to the other sex. Submission and obedience belong to every being in the universe, except the great Master of the whole. Nor is it a degrading peculiarity to our sex, to be under human authority. Whenever one class of human beings, derive from another the benefits of support and protection, they must pay its equivalent, obedience. Thus, while we receive these benefits from our parents, we are all, without distinction of sex, under their authority; when we receive them from the government of our country, we must obey our rulers; and when our sex take the obligations of marriage, and receive protection and support from the other, it is reasonable, that we too should yield obedience. Yet is neither the child, nor the subject, nor the wife, under human authority, but in subservience to the divine. Our highest responsibility is to God, and our highest interest is to please him; therefore, to secure this interest, should our education be directed.

Neither would I be understood to mean, that our sex should not seek to make themselves agreeable to the other. The errour complained of, is that the taste of men, whatever it might happen to be, has been made a standard for the formation of the female character. In whatever we do, it is of the utmost importance, that the rule, by which we work, be perfect. For if otherwise, what is it, but to err upon principle? A system of education, which leads one class of human beings to consider the approbation of another, as their highest object, teaches, that the rule of their conduct should be the will of beings, imperfect and erring like themselves, rather than the will of God, which is the only standard of perfection.

Having now considered female education, both in theory and practice, and seen, that in its present state, it is in fact a thing "without form and void," the mind is naturally led to inquire after a remedy for the evils it has been contemplating. Can individuals furnish this remedy? It has heretofore been left to them, and we have seen the consequence. If education is a business, which might naturally prosper, if left to individual exertion, why have legislatures intermeddled with it at all? if it is not, why do they make their daughters illegitimates, and bestow all their cares upon their sons?

It is the duty of a government, to do all in its power to promote the present and future prosperity of the nation, over which it is placed. This prosperity will depend on the character of its citizens. The characters of these will be formed by their mothers; and it is through the mothers, that the government can control the characters of its future citizens, to form them such as will ensure their country's prosperity. If this is the case, then it is the duty of our present legislators to begin now, to form the characters of the next generation, by controling that of the females, who are to be their mothers, while it is yet with them a season of improvement.

But should the conclusion be almost admitted, that

our sex too are the legitimate children of the legislature; and, that it is their duty to afford us a share of their paternal bounty; the phantom of a college-learned lady, would be ready to rise up, and destroy every good resolution, which the admission of this truth would naturally produce in our favour.

To shew that it is not a masculine education which is here recommended, and to afford a definite view of the manner in which a female institution might possess the respectability, permanency, and uniformity of operation of those appropriated to males; and yet differ from them, so as to be adapted to that difference of character and duties, to which the softer sex should be formed, is the object of the following imperfect

SKETCH OF A FEMALE SEMINARY.

From considering the deficiencies in boarding schools, much may be learned, with regard to what would be needed, for the prosperity and usefulness of a public seminary for females.

I. There would be needed a building, with commodious rooms for lodging and recitation, apartments for the reception of apparatus, and for the accommodation of the domestic department.

II. A library, containing books on the various subjects in which the pupils were to receive instruction; musical instruments, some good paintings, to form the taste and serve as models for the execution of those who were to be instructed in that art; maps, globes, and a small collection of philosophical apparatus.

III. A judicious board of trust, competent and desirous to promote its interests, would in a female, as in a male literary institution, be the corner stone of its prosperity. On this board it would depend to provide,

IV. Suitable instruction. This article may be subdivided under four heads.
1. Religious and Moral.
2. Literary.
3. Domestic.
4. Ornamental.

1. Religious and Moral. A regular attention to religious duties would, of course be required of the pupils by the laws of the institution. The trustees would be careful to appoint no instructors, who would not teach religion and morality, both by their example, and by leading the minds of the pupils to perceive, that these constitute the true end of all education. It would be desirable, that the young ladies should spend a part of their Sabbaths in hearing discourses relative to the peculiar duties of their sex. The evidences of Christianity, and moral philosophy, would constitute a part of their studies.

2. Literary Instruction. To make an exact enumeration of the branches of literature, which might be taught, would be impossible, unless the time of the pupils' continuance at the seminary, and the requisites for entrance, were previously fixed. Such an enumeration would be tedious, nor do I conceive that it would be at all promotive of my object. The difficulty complained of, is not, that we are at a loss what sciences we ought to learn, but that we have not proper advantages to learn any. Many writers have given us excellent advice with regard to what we should be taught, but no legislature has provided us the means of instruction. Not however, to pass lightly over this fundamental part of education, I will mention one or two of the less obvious branches of science, which, I conceive should engage the youthful attention of my sex.

It is highly important, that females should be conversant with those studies, which will lead them to understand the operations of the human mind. The chief use to which the philosophy of the mind can be applied, is to regulate education by its rules. The ductile mind of the child is intrusted to the mother: and she ought to have every possible assistance, in acquiring a knowledge of this noble material, on which it is her business to operate, that she may best understand how to mould it to its most excellent form.

Natural philosophy has not often been taught to our sex. Yet why should we be kept in ignorance of the great machinery of nature, and left to the vulgar notion, that nothing is curious but what deviates from her common course? If mothers were acquainted with this science, they would communicate very many of its principles to their children in early youth. From the bursting of an egg buried in the fire, I have heard an intelligent mother, lead her prattling inquirer, to understand the cause of the earthquake. But how often does the mother, from ignorance on this subject, give her child the most erroneous and contracted views of the causes of natural phenomena; views, which, though he may afterwards learn to be false, are yet, from the laws of association, ever ready to return, unless the active powers of the mind are continually upon the alert to keep them out. A knowledge of natural philosophy is calculated to heighten the moral taste, by bringing to view the majesty and beauty of order and design; and to enliven piety, by enabling the mind more clearly to perceive, throughout the manifold works of God, that wisdom, in which he hath made them all.

In some of the sciences proper for our sex, the books, written for the other, would need alteration; because, in some they presuppose more knowledge than female pupils would possess; in others, they have parts not particularly interesting to our sex, and omit subjects immediately relating to their pursuits. There would likewise be needed, for a female seminary, some works, which I believe are no where extant, such as a systematic treatise on housewifery.

3. Domestic Instruction should be considered important in a female seminary. It is the duty of our sex to regulate the internal concerns of every family; and unless they be properly qualified to discharge this duty, whatever may be their literary or ornamental attainments, they cannot be expected to make either good wives, good mothers, or good mistresses of families: and if they are none of these, they must be bad members of society; for it is by promoting or destroying the comfort and prosperity of their own families, that females serve or injure the community. To superintend the domestic department, there should be a respectable lady, experienced in the best methods of housewifery, and acquainted with propriety of dress and manners. Under her tuition the pupils ought to be placed for a certain length of time every morning. A spirit of neatness and order should here be treated as a virtue, and the contrary, if excessive and incorrigible, be punished with expulsion. There might be a gradation of employment in the domestic department, according to the length of time the pupils had remained at the institution. The older scholars might then assist the superintendant in instructing the younger, and the whole be so arranged, that each pupil might have advantages to become a good domestic manager by the time she has completed her studies.

This plan would afford a healthy exercise. It would prevent that estrangement from domestic duties, which would be likely to take place in a length of time devoted to study, with those, to whom they were previously familiar; and would accustom those to them, who, from ignorance, might otherwise put at hazard their own happiness, and the prosperity of their families.

These objects might doubtless be effected by a scheme of domestic instruction; and probably others of no inconsiderable importance. It is believed, that housewifery might be greatly improved, by being taught, not only in practice, but in theory. Why may it not be reduced to a system, as well as other arts? There are right ways of performing its various operations; and there are reasons why those ways are right; and why may not rules be formed, their reasons collected; and the whole be digested into a system to guide the learner's practice?

It is obvious, that theory alone, can never make a good artist; and it is equally obvious, that practice unaided by theory, can never correct errors, but must establish them. If I should perform any thing in a wrong manner all my life, and teach my children to perform it in the same manner, still, through my life and theirs, it would be wrong. Without alteration there can be no improvement; but how are we to alter, so as to improve, if we are ignorant of the principles of our art, with which we should compare our practice, and by which we should regulate it?

In the present state of things, it is not to be expected, that any material improvements in housewifery should be made. There being no uniformity of method, prevailing among different housewives, of course, the communications from one to another, are not much more likely to improve the art, than a communication, between two mechanics of different trades, would be, to improve each in his respective occupation. But should a system of principles be philosophically arranged, and taught, both in theory and by practice, to a large number of females, whose minds were expanded and strengthened by a course of literary instruction, those among them, of an investigating turn, would, when they commenced housekeepers, consider their domestic operations as a series of experiments, which either proved or refuted the system previously taught. They would then converse together like those, who practise a common art, and improve each other by their observations and experiments; and they would also be capable of improving the system, by detecting its errors, and by making additions of new principles and better modes of practice.

4. The Ornamental branches, which I should recommend for a female seminary, are drawing and painting, elegant penmanship, music, and the grace of motion. Needle-work is not here mentioned. The best style of useful needle-work should either be taught in the domestic department, or made a qualification for entrance; and I consider that useful, which may contribute to the decoration of a lady's person, or the convenience and neatness of her family. But the use of the needle, for other purposes than these, as it affords little to assist in the formation of the character, I should regard as a waste of time.

The grace of motion, must be learnt chiefly from instruction in dancing. Other advantages besides that of a graceful carriage, might be derived from such instruction, if the lessons were judiciously timed. Exercise is needful to the health, and recreation to the cheerfulness and contentment of youth. Female youth could not be allowed to range unrestrained, to seek amusement for themselves. If it was entirely prohibited, they would be driven to seek it by stealth; which would lead them to many improprieties of conduct, and would have a pernicious effect upon their general character, by inducing a habit of treading forbidden paths. The alternative that remains is to provide them with proper recreation, which, after the confinement of the day, they might enjoy under the eye of their instructors. Dancing is exactly suited to this purpose, as also to that of exercise; for perhaps in no way, can so much healthy exercise be taken in so short a time. It has besides, this advantage over other amusements, that it affords nothing to excite the bad passions; but, on the contrary, its effects are, to soften the mind, to banish its animosities, and to open it to social impressions.

It may be said, that dancing would dissipate the attention, and estrange it from study. Balls would doubtless have this effect; but let dancing be practised every day, by youth of the same sex, without change of place, dress, or company, and under the eye of those, whom they are accustomed to obey, and it would excite no more emotion, than any other exercise or amusement, but in degree, as it is of itself more pleasant. But it must ever be a grateful exercise to youth, as it is one, to which nature herself prompts them, at the sound of animating music.

It has been doubted, whether painting and music should be taught to young ladies, because much time is requisite to bring them to any considerable degree of perfection, and they are not immediately useful. Though these objections have weight, yet they are founded on too limited a view of the objects of education. They leave out the important consideration of forming the character. I should not consider it an essential point, that the music of a lady's piano should rival that of her master's; or that her drawing room should be decorated with her own paintings, rather than those of others; but it is the intrinsic advantage, which she might derive from the refinement of herself, that would induce me to recommend to her, an attention to those elegant pursuits. The harmony of sound, has a tendency to produce a correspondent harmony of soul; and that art, which obliges us to study nature, in order to imitate her, often enkindles the latent spark of taste—of sensibility for her beauties, till it glows to adoration for their author, and a refined love of all his works.

V. There would be needed, for a female, as well as for a male seminary, a system of laws and regulations, so arranged, that both the instructors and pupils would know their duty; and thus, the whole business, move with regularity and uniformity.

The laws of the institution would be chiefly directed, to regulate the pupil's qualifications for entrance, the kind and order of their studies, their behaviour while at the institution, the term allotted for the completion of their studies, the punishments to be inflicted on offenders and the rewards or honours, to be bestowed on the virtuous and diligent.

The direct rewards or honors, used to stimulate the ambition of students in colleges, are first, the certificate or diploma, which each receives, who passes successfully through the term allotted to his collegiate studies; and secondly, the appointments to perform certain parts in public exhibitions, which are bestowed by the faculty, as rewards for superior scholarship. The first of these modes is admissible into a female seminary; the second is not; as public speaking forms no part of female education. The want of this mode, might, however, be supplied by examinations judiciously conducted. The leisure and inclination of both instructors and scholars, would combine to produce a thorough preparation for these; for neither would have any other public test of the success of their labors. Persons of both sexes would attend. The less entertaining parts, might be enlivened by interludes, where the pupils in painting and music, would display their several improvements. Such examinations, would stimulate the instructors to give their scholars more attention, by which the leading facts and principles of their studies, would be more clearly understood, and better remembered. The ambition excited among the pupils, would operate, without placing the instructors under the necessity of making distinctions among them, which are so apt to be considered as invidious; and which are, in our male seminaries, such fruitful sources of disaffection.

Perhaps the term allotted for the routine of study at the seminary, might be three years. The pupils, probably, would not be fitted to enter, till about the age of fourteen. Whether they attended to all, or any of the ornamental branches, should be left optional with the parents or guardians. Those who were to be instructed in them, should be entered for a longer term, but if this was a subject of previous calculation, no confusion would arise from it. The routine of the exercises being established by the laws of the institution, would be uniform, and publicly known; and those, who were previously acquainted with the branches first taught, might enter the higher classes; nor would those who entered the lowest, be obliged to remain during the three years. Thus the term of remaining at the institution, might be either one, two, three, four, or more years; and that, without interfering with the regularity and uniformity of its proceedings.

The writer has now given a sketch of her plan. She has by no means expressed all the ideas, which occurred to her concerning it. She wished to be as concise as possible, and yet afford conviction, that it is practicable, to organize a system of female education, which shall possess the permanency, uniformity of operation, and respectability of our male institutions; and yet differ from them, so as to be adapted, to that difference of character, and duties, to which early instruction should form the softer sex.

It now remains, to enquire more particularly, what would be the benefits resulting from such a system.

BENEFITS OF FEMALE SEMINARIES.

In inquiring, concerning the benefits of the plan proposed, I shall proceed upon the supposition, that female seminaries will be patronized throughout our country.

Nor is this altogether a visionary supposition. If one seminary should be well organized, its advantages would be found so great, that others would soon be instituted; and, that sufficient patronage can be found to put one in operation, may be presumed from its reasonableness, and from the public opinion, with regard to the present mode of female education. It is from an intimate acquaintance, with those parts of our country, whose education is said to flourish most, that the writer has drawn her picture of the present state of female instruction; and she knows, that she is not alone, in perceiving or deploring its faults. Her sentiments are shared by many an enlightened parent of a daughter, who has received a boarding school education. Counting on the promise of her childhood, the father had anticipated her maturity, as combining what is excellent in mind, with what is elegant in manners. He spared no expense that education might realize to him, the image of his imagination. His daughter returned from boarding school, improved in fashionable airs, and expert in manufacturing fashionable toys; but, in her conversation, he sought in vain, for that refined and fertile mind, which he had fondly expected. Aware that his disappointment has its source in a defective education, he looks with anxiety on his other daughters, whose minds, like lovely buds, are beginning to open. Where shall he find a genial soil, in which he may place them to expand? Shall he provide them male instructors?— Then the graces of their persons and manners, and whatever forms the distinguishing charm of the feminine character, they cannot be expected to acquire.— Shall he give them a private tutoress? She will have been educated at the boarding school, and his daughters will have the faults of its instruction second-handed. Such is now the dilemma of many parents; and it is one, from which they cannot be extricated by their individual exertions. May not then the only plan, which promises to relieve them, expect their vigorous support.

Let us now proceed to inquire, what benefits would result from the establishment of female seminaries.

They would constitute a grade of public education, superior to any yet known in the history of our sex; and through them, the lower grades of female instruction might be controlled. The influence of public seminaries, over these, would operate in two ways; first, by requiring certain qualifications for entrance; and secondly, by furnishing instructresses, initiated in their modes of teaching, and imbued with their maxims.

Female seminaries might be expected to have important and happy effects, on common schools in general; and in the manner of operating on these, would probably place the business of teaching children, in hands now nearly useless to society; and take it from those, whose services the state wants in many other ways.

That nature designed for our sex the care of children, she has made manifest, by mental, as well as physical indications. She has given us, in a greater degree than men, the gentle arts of insinuation, to soften their minds, and fit them to receive impressions; a greater quickness of invention to vary modes of teaching to different dispositions; and more patience to make repeated efforts. There are many females of ability, to whom the business of instructing children is highly acceptable, and, who would devote all their faculties to their occupation. They would have no higher pecuniary object to engage their attention, and their reputation as instructors they would consider as important; whereas, whenever able and enterprizing men, engage in this business, they consider it, merely as a temporary employment, to further some other object, to the attainment of which, their best thoughts and calculations are all directed. If then women were properly fitted by instruction, they would be likely to teach children better than the other sex; they could afford to do it cheaper; and those men who would otherwise be engaged in this employment, might be at liberty to add to the wealth of the nation, by any of those thousand occupations, from which women are necessarily debarred.

But the females, who taught children, would have been themselves instructed either immediately or indirectly by the seminaries. Hence through these, the government might exercise an intimate, and most benificial control over common schools. Any one, who has turned his attention to this subject, must be aware, that there is great room for improvement in these, both as to the modes of teaching, and the things taught; and what method could be devised so likely to effect this improvement, as to prepare by instruction, a class of individuals, whose interest, leisure, and natural talents, would combine to make them pursue it with ardour. Such a class of individuals would be raised up, by female seminaries. And therefore they would be likely to have highly important and happy effects on common schools.

It is believed, that such institutions, would tend to prolong, or perpetuate our excellent government.

An opinion too generally prevails, that our present form of government, though good, cannot be permanent. Other republics have failed, and the historian and philosopher have told us, that nations are like individuals; that, at their birth, they receive the seeds of their decline and dissolution. Here deceived by a false analagy, we receive an apt illustration of particular facts, for a general truth. The existence of nations, cannot, in strictness, be compared with the duration of animate life; for by the operation of physical causes, this, after a certain length of time, must cease: but the existence of nations, is prolonged by the succession of one generation to another, and there is no physical cause, to prevent this succession's going on, in a peaceable manner, under a good government, till the end of time. We must then look to other causes, than necessity, for the decline and fall of former republics. If we could discover these causes, and seasonably prevent their operation, then might our latest posterity enjoy the same happy government, with which we are blessed; or if but in part, then might the triumph of tyranny, be delayed, and a few more generations be free.

Permit me then to ask the enlightened politician of my country, whether amidst his researches for these causes, he cannot discover one, in the neglect, which free governments, in common with others, have shown, to whatever regarded the formation of the female character.

In those great republics, which have fallen of themselves, the loss of republican manners and virtues, has been the invariable precursor, of their loss of the republican form of government. But is it not in the power of our sex, to give society its tone, both as to manners and morals? And if such is the extent of female influence, is it wonderful, that republics have failed, when they calmly suffered that influence, to become enlisted in favour of luxuries and follies, wholly incompatible with the existence of freedom?

It may be said, that the depravation of morals and manners, can be traced to the introduction of wealth, as its cause. But wealth will be introduced; even the iron laws of Lycurgus could not prevent it. Let us then inquire, if means may not be devised, to prevent its bringing with it the destruction of public virtue. May not these means be found in education?—in implanting, in early youth, habits, that may counteract the temptations, to which, through the influence of wealth, mature age will be exposed? and in giving strength and expansion to the mind, that it may comprehend, and prize those principles, which teach the rigid performance of duty? Education, it may be said, has been tried as a preservative of national purity. But was it applied to every exposed part of the body politic? For if any part has been left within the pestilential atmosphere of wealth, without this preservative, then that part becoming corrupted, would communicate the contagion to the whole; and if so, then has the experiment, whether education may not preserve public virtue, never yet been fairly tried. Such a part has been left in all former experiments. Females have been exposed to the contagion of wealth without the preservative of a good education; and they constitute that part of the body politic, least endowed by nature to resist, most to communicate it. Nay, not merely have they been left without the defence of a good education, but their corruption has been accelerated by a bad one. The character of women of rank and wealth has been, and in the old governments of Europe now is, all that this statement would lead us to expect. Not content with doing nothing to promote their country's welfare, like pampered children, they revel in its prosperity, and scatter it to the winds, with a wanton profusion: and still worse,—they empoison its source, by diffusing a contempt for useful labour. To court pleasure their business,—within her temple, in defiance of the laws of God and man, they have erected the idol fashion; and upon her altar, they sacrifice, with shameless rites, whatever is sacred to virtue or religion. Not the strongest ties of nature,—not even maternal love can restrain them! Like the worshipper of Moloch, the mother while yet yearning over the new born babe, tears it from the bosom, which God has swelled with nutrition for its support, and casts it remorseless from her, the victim of her unhallowed devotion!

But while, with an anguished heart, I thus depict the crimes of my sex, let not the other stand by and smile. Reason declares, that you are guiltier than we. You are our natural guardians,—our brothers,—our fathers, and our rulers. You know that our ductile minds, readily take the impressions of education. Why then have you neglected our education? Why have you looked with lethargic indifference, on circumstances ruinous to the formation of our characters, which you might have controlled?

But it may be said, the observations here made, cannot be applied to any class of females in our country. True, they cannot yet; and if they could, it would be useless to make them; for when the females of any country have become thus debased, then, is that country so corrupted, that nothing, but the awful judgments of heaven, can arrest its career of vice. But it cannot be denied, that our manners are verging towards those described; and the change, though gradual, has not been slow: already do our daughters listen with surprise, when we tell them of the republican simplicity of our mothers. But our manners are not as yet so altered, but that, throughout our country, they are still marked with republican virtues.

The inquiry, to which these remarks have conducted us is this—What is offered by the plan of female education, here proposed, which may teach, or preserve, among females of wealthy families, that purity of manners, which is allowed, to be so essential to national prosperity, and so necessary, to the existence of a republican government.

1. Females, by having their understandings cultivated, their reasoning powers developed and strengthened, may be expected to act more from the dictates of reason, and less from those of fashion and caprice.

2. With minds thus strengthened they would be taught systems of morality, enforced by the sanctions of religion; and they might be expected to acquire juster and more enlarged views of their duty, and stronger and higher motives to its performance.

3. This plan of education, offers all that can be done to preserve female youth from a contempt of useful labour. The pupils would become accustomed to it, in conjunction with the high objects of literature, and the elegant pursuits of the fine arts; and it is to be hoped

that both from habit and association, they might in future life, regard it as respectable.

To this it may be added, that if housewifery could be raised to a regular art, and taught upon philosophical principles, it would become a higher and more interesting occupation; and ladies of fortune, like wealthy agriculturalists, might find, that to regulate their business, was an agreeable employment.

4. The pupils might be expected to acquire a taste for moral and intellectual pleasures, which would buoy them above a passion for show and parade, and which would make them seek to gratify the natural love of superiority, by endeavouring to excel others in intrinsic merit, rather than in the extrinsic frivolities of dress, furniture, and equipage.

5. By being enlightened in moral philosophy, and in that, which teaches the operations of the mind, females would be enabled to perceive the nature and extent, of that influence, which they possess over their children, and the obligation, which this lays them under, to watch the formation of their characters with unceasing vigilance, to become their instructors, to devise plans for their improvement, to weed out the vices from their minds, and to implant and foster the virtues. And surely, there is that in the maternal bosom, which, when its pleadings shall be aided by education, will overcome the seductions of wealth and fashion, and will lead the mother, to seek her happiness in communing with her children, and promoting their welfare, rather than in a heartless intercourse, with the votaries of pleasure: especially, when with an expanded mind, she extends her views to futurity, and sees her care to her offspring rewarded by peace of conscience, the blessings of her family, the prosperity of her country, and finally with everlasting happiness to herself and them.

Thus, laudable objects and employments, would be furnished for the great body of females, who are not kept by poverty from excesses. But among these, as among the other sex, will be found master spirits, who must have pre-eminence, at whatever price they acquire it. Domestic life cannot hold these, because they prefer to be infamous, rather than obscure. To leave such, without any virtuous road to eminence, is unsafe to community; for not unfrequently, are the secret springs of revolution, set in motion by their intrigues. Such aspiring minds, we will regulate, by education, we will remove obstructions to the course of literature, which has heretofore been their only honorable way to distinction; and we offer them a new object, worthy of their ambition; to govern, and improve the seminaries for their sex.

In calling on my patriotic countrymen, to effect so noble an object, the consideration of national glory, should not be overlooked. Ages have rolled away;—barbarians have trodden the weaker sex beneath their feet;—tyrants have robbed us of the present light of heaven, and fain would take its future. Nations, calling themselves polite, have made us the fancied idols of a ridiculous worship, and we have repaid them with ruin for their folly. But where is that wise and heroic country, which has considered, that our rights are sacred, though we cannot defend them? that tho' a weaker, we are an essential part of the body politic, whose corruption or improvement must affect the whole? and which, having thus considered, has sought to give us by education, that rank in the scale of being, to which our importance entitles us? History shows not that country. It shows many, whose legislatures have sought to improve their various vegetable productions, and their breeds of useful brutes; but none, whose public councils have made it an object of their deliberations, to improve the character of their women. Yet though history lifts not her finger to such an one, anticipation does. She points to a nation, which, having thrown off the shackles of authority and precedent, shrinks not from schemes of improvement, because other nations have never attempted them; but which, in its pride of independence, would rather lead than follow, in the march of human improvement: a nation, wise and magnanimous to plan, enterprising to undertake, and rich in resources to execute. Does not every American exult that this country is his own? And who knows how great and good a race of men, may yet arise from the forming hand of mothers, enlightened by the bounty of that beloved country,—to defend her liberties,—to plan her future improvement,—and to raise her to unparalleled glory?

UNITED STATES BUREAU OF EDUCATION.
CIRCULAR OF INFORMATION NO. 4, 1900.

CONTRIBUTIONS TO AMERICAN EDUCATIONAL HISTORY.
EDITED BY HERBERT B. ADAMS.

No. 29.   [*Whole Number 265*

HISTORY OF EDUCATION

IN

VERMONT.

BY

GEORGE GARY BUSH, Ph. D.

MRS. EMMA WILLARD'S LIFE AND WORK IN MIDDLEBURY.

Prepared originally for the Emma Willard Society of New York by Ezra Brainerd, L.L.D., President of Middlebury, College, 1885-1908

Mrs. Emma Willard is known as the pioneer in the great movement of the nineteenth century for the higher education of woman. To say that she had a genius for teaching, that she devised improved methods, that she wrote admirable text-books, and that she impressed her own high ideals upon the characters of her pupils is indeed great praise.

But it is a still greater glory to have started a movement which has revolutionized the ideas of the civilized world on the subject of woman's education, a movement which has culminated in the founding of grand colleges exclusively for women and in the admission of women to older colleges on equal terms with men. For it is not too much to say that Wellesley and Vassar and their sister institutions on either side the Atlantic are the fair fruitage, in time, of those seminal ideas so ably set forth in Mrs. Willard's Plan of Female Education.

It is interesting to study the origin of such a great movement; it is like tracing some noble river upward to its sources in the distant mountains. Let it be our pleasant task to search out, as far as possible, the influences that shaped Mrs. Willard's career as an educator. In so doing we shall find that the formative period of her life was the twelve years spent in Middlebury—a period passed over too cursorily in Dr. Lord's biography. The fresh interest in this truly great woman, awakened by the Emma Willard associations of the country, is an additional reason for considering more in detail the incidents of this portion of her life and for inquiring into the moral forces which called forth her grand ideas regarding the scope of woman's education.

We should, as a preliminary, call to mind briefly the circumstances of her early life in Connecticut, her excellent parentage, the beautiful home life of her childhood, her two years of earnest study under Dr. Wells, her brilliant success as a teacher at the early age of 17. These facts help us to picture the bright, noble-hearted woman who, at the age of 20, came in 1807 to take charge of the female academy at Middlebury.

The influences that shaped her character in her new home were from three sources. Let us speak first of her social surroundings.

The early inhabitants of Middlebury were noted for their enterprise and intelligence. Up to the close of the Revolutionary war the Champlain Valley had been for centuries the arena of savage warfare. But as soon as the cessation of hostilities would permit these fertile lands were rapidly settled by a vigorous and high-minded class of young men and women from the best families of Connecticut. There was in Middlebury an unusually large number of educated men, graduates of Yale and Dartmouth and Brown. Of their interest in religion and taste in architecture they have left a striking monument in the church edifice, that is still standing, with its beautiful groined arches and its graceful steeple, after the Christopher Wren style. Their devotion to the cause of education is evinced by their establishment, before the beginning of the present century, of three distinct institutions of learning—the grammar school, the female academy, and the college. The elder President Dwight, of Yale, who made three visits to the town prior to 1810, has recorded in his books of travels his high appreciation of the character of the people and of their educational work. Mrs. Willard herself, then Miss Emma Hart, has given emphatic testimony to the same effect. In a letter to her parents, written during the first year of her residence, she says:

> I find society in a high state of cultivation, much more than any other place I was ever in. The beaux here are, the greater part of them, men of collegiate education. * * * Among the older ladies there are some whose manners and conversation would dignify duchesses.

If our limits would permit, we might speak in particular of some of these excellent men and women whose society Miss Hart thus enjoyed. It was her privilege to know the Hon. Horatio Seymour, afterwards for twelve years United States Senator, a man who was earnest from the first in the cause of woman's education, and who gave the land on which was erected in 1802 the "Female Academy," one of the very first school edifices in the country built especially for women. She knew also the Rev. Dr. Merrill, who, on graduating from Dartmouth in 1801, had won the valedictory over his illustrious classmate Daniel Webster, and who for thirty-seven years was pastor of the Congregational church and a recognized leader throughout the State in matters of education and religion. She knew also Dr. Henry Davis, president of the college, who was eminent for his talents and eloquence and personal address, who was in 1817, on the death of Dr. Dwight, elected president of Yale College, and who reflected no small honor on Middlebury by declining the appointment. With these men and others of scarcely less character, not yet famous, but in the vigor of early manhood, Miss Hart, the young preceptress of the Female Academy, was called to associate. Her letters and journal show how deeply interested she was in her new life. She has an intense relish for agreeable society; she attends parties and balls during the week, and four meetings on Sunday. She drinks deep draughts of the joyous cup of youth and health. But her strong brain never becomes giddy; there is too much of the Puritan seriousness in her veins. She keeps up her studies in history; she writes poetry; she paints; she criticises sermons; and withal conducts a school for young ladies with constantly increasing reputation.

The building where this school was held is still standing. It has been unused for years, but is guarded with religious care by its present owner, a son-in-law of Horatio Seymour. The whole of the second story was one large room, warmed only by an open fireplace in the north end. For in those days, as Lowell tells us:

> There warn't no stoves (tell comfort died)
> To bake ye to a puddin'.

But a fireplace did not always bring comfort to the schoolroom during the severe cold of that Vermont winter. The north wind at times would whistle around the building and penetrate the schoolroom until they could endure the cold no longer. The tact of the schoolmistress was equal to the emergency. She would then (so she writes in a letter to Judge Swift) call her girls to the floor and arrange them two and two in a long row for a contradance; and while those who could sing would strike up some stirring tune she, with one of the girls for a partner, would lead down the dance and soon have them all in rapid motion. Afterwards they would return to their school exercises.

But in two years she closed her connection with the female academy. On the 10th day of August, 1809, she was married to Dr. John Willard. And this brings us to the second phase of her Middlebury life, and to consider the influences of this marriage upon her after career.

Dr. Willard was twenty-eight years the senior of his wife, but nowhere in the annals of biography can we find a married life more happy than theirs was from first to last. From several letters we are permitted to see how intimate was the union of heart and soul between the two. As we read them there arises before us the fair picture of the enthusiastic young wife, studying to make herself less unworthy of the good and wise man who had enthroned her in his heart. In his absence she delves into the dry books of his medical library, to prepare herself to sympathize with him in his passionate attachment for these old authors. He is delighted to find her kindled into his enthusiasm and able to discuss with him intelligently questions of physiology and medicine. Then at another time she takes up the study of geometry. Dr. Willard has a nephew in college who lives with them— his namesake, afterwards for many years judge of the supreme court in New York. One vacation she takes up his Euclid and reads on, proposition after proposition, fascinated with the study. She thinks she understands it; but the general belief in the incapacity of "the female mind" for mathematics causes misgivings, until she submits herself to her nephew for examination, and he pronounces her learning correct. The same thirst for knowledge afterwards leads her to take up natural philosophy and to study Paley's Moral Philosophy and Locke's Essay concerning Human Understanding. Most men in those days (perhaps some in our day) would have discouraged a wife in such ambitious and unfeminine studies. Not so Dr. Willard. His generous heart was pleased with her efforts after intellectual culture, and he was proud of her achievements. There began to dawn upon his mind new views of woman's mental capacity, and a disposition to take her part against man's lordly assumption of superiority. It would be a great error to imagine that during the early years of her married life Mrs. Willard was engrossed in intellectual pursuits. These were only her diversions; domestic duties occupied the greater portion of her time. Her son was born in 1810. Dr. Willard was away from home much of the time, and the charge of the household

and the farm devolved upon the young wife, who performed these
duties with care and prudence. An interesting letter, quoted by Dr.
Lord, informs her husband that "the winter apples are gathered; the
cider is made (23 barrels); the potatoes are nearly all in; the buck-
wheat is gathered," and so on through a long list of homely duties.
Surely here was

> A creature not too bright or good
> For human nature's daily food.

So passed another period in the life of this great woman, a period
filled with the happy experiences of wifehood and motherhood. But
clouds after a while appeared in their bright sky; God was leading
them on to a higher stage in their life work.

Dr. Willard was a man of property and of high social position at
the time of his marriage to Miss Hart. He owned several small farms
in the vicinity of Middlebury; he had just built an elegant brick house
on Main street, now occupied by Mrs. Charles Linsley. He had been
a successful politician; he was chairman of the central committee of
the Republican party, was appointed marshal of the District of Vermont by Jefferson in 1801, and was one of the directors of the Vermont
State Bank. His financial embarrassment largely grew out of his
connection with this bank through a romantic incident that is not generally known. In the summer of 1812 an adroit burglary was com-
mitted on the banking house in Middlebury. It was entered by a
false key, and a large sum of money was taken without leaving any
signs of violence or disorder. Of course the directors very soon dis-
covered the fact of the burglary; but it was not so obvious to the public, and the directors were called upon to account for the missing
funds. The legislature was led to adopt harsh measures for their
prosecution, and after a trial before the supreme court judgment was
rendered against the supposed delinquents for over $28,000. The
greater part of this claim, it is true, was remitted by a subsequent
legislature; and in after years the discovery of the false key in the
attic of a certain house fully vindicated the innocence of the directors.
But the records of the town show that the liens of the Vermont State
Bank on the real estate of John Willard were removed only after
many years.

But the heroism of the devoted wife was equal to the occasion.
She would return to the work in which she had achieved such brilliant
success before her happy marriage. She would open a boarding school
for girls in her own house. The project must have been humiliating to
the mind of Dr. Willard. Only a loving confidence in his wife could
have secured his consent; but when he gave it he set himself to work
with her, heart and soul, to the end.

It should be remembered that when Mrs. Willard first opened her
school in 1814 her "plan" was altogether undeveloped. She had none

of those ambitious projects for the higher education of woman which afterwards animated her. Her sole object, as she distinctly says, was to assist her husband in his pecuniary affairs. It was while walking lovingly in the pathway of domestic duty that the Lord led her into the wider field of her life's mission. It remains for us then to consider this third stage in her novitiate, the light that came to her through her new experiences in teaching.

Mrs. Willard's home in Middlebury was almost under the shadow of Middlebury College. The college campus was just across the street from her house. She heard from hour to hour through the day the call of the bell to chapel or to recitation. For four years she listened to reports of college life and work from the nephew, who sat at her table while a student. When she opened her new school she taught at first the usual round of light and superficial studies that the age had prescribed for "females." But "my neighborhood to Middlebury College," she writes, "made me bitterly feel the disparity in educational facilities between the sexes." She had already made private excursions into the realms of solid learning, forbidden to her sex, and she was profoundly conscious of woman's capacity to understand all that was highest and best in the reaches of human thought. Why should the sister be deprived of the intellectual culture that is offered to the brother? Why will not the companionship of wedded life be purer and stronger if the mental training of the wife is comparable with that of the husband? Why will not the mother give to the world nobler sons and daughers if her own character be strengthened and refined by the highest education? These are hackneyed questions to-day, but they were new to the world when in 1815 they first throbbed in the brain of Mrs. Willard.

Then the further question came: Could she herself effect this great change for woman? She heard the divine call; should she be disobedient to the heavenly vision? The cause was so just, so humane, so practicable, that surely if she could advocate it before governors and legislators she might effect the desired reform. Still the project seemed presumptuous, so that she hesitated to entertain it; she concealed it for a while even from her husband, though knowing that he sympathized with her in her desires for the better education of woman.

But the absorbing, unborn purpose of her soul she could not long keep from the confidence of her husband. How he received her confidence she shall tell us in her own fervid words: "He entered into the full spirit of my views with a disinterested zeal for that sex, whom, as he believed, his own had injuriously neglected. With an affection more generous and disinterested than ever man before felt, he, in his later life, sought my elevation, indifferent to his own. Possessing on the whole an opinion of me more favorable than any other human being ever will have, and, thus encouraging me to dare much, he yet knew my weaknesses, and fortified me against them."

Mrs. Willard now addresses herself to the task of elaborating "A plan for improving female education." It was the slow work of two or three years. It was written and rewritten seven times; fully three-fourths of the original matter was finally rejected. She was meanwhile testing some of her theories by experiments, so far as her limited resources would permit. She formed a class in moral philosophy, and another in the philosophy of the mind, taking Locke's great work as a text-book. The professors of the college were fearlessly invited to attend her examinations, and to witness the proofs that "the female mind" could appreciate and apprehend the solid studies of the college course. She desired, in turn, to attend the examinations of the young men, to learn how they were conducted, and to see what attainments in scholarship were made in college. It is humiliating to think that this privilege was refused, President Davis considering that it would not be a safe precedent, and that it would be unbecoming in her to attend. But let us not blame too severely this stanch defender of the proprieties; he was simply guarding well-bred society from a terrible nervous shock.

These were the rough ways of the world—till now.

Mrs. Willard was for some time perplexed to find a suitable name for her ideal institution. It would never do to call it a "college," for the proposal to send young ladies to college would strike everyone as an absurdity. She has told us how she finally hit upon a suitable name. "I heard Dr. Merrill pray for 'our seminaries of learning.' I said, I have it—I will call it a female seminary. That word, while it is high as the highest, is also low as the lowest, and will not create a jealousy that we mean to intrude upon the province of the men." And so the word came afterwards into general use to designate the higher grade of schools for girls.

We can not enter into any detailed discussion of the "plan," as it was finally published in 1818. In many respects it is open to criticism, if we judge it by the higher standards of the present. The seventy-five years since passed have seen wonderful changes in our ideas regarding woman's education and woman's work—thanks to the publication of this same treatise. It is of the nature of a plea, and she is evidently cautious about asking too much, for fear she may lose all. Still we must regard it as a wonderful document—the Magna Charta of the rights of woman in matters of education.

It was addressed to a State legislature, for Mrs. Willard rightly judged that the equipment of her ideal institution could not be furnished by private means, and that it could be properly managed and perpetuated only by a legal board of trustees. Those were not the days of large private fortunes and still less of princely donations to institutions of public charity or of general education. Mrs. Willard felt that her only recourse was to secure the State patronage which was at the disposal of patriotic lawmakers. Of the reasons that led her to apply to the legislature of New York, of her grievous disappointment after years of patient effort and waiting, of the brilliant success which she finally achieved, principally through her own great personality, it is foreign to my present purpose to speak. These things are more clearly matters of history than the obscure events of her early life in Middlebury.

Let me simply add in closing that to-day the spirit of her teachings has thoroughly permeated the institutions of the town where her great work originated. The ladies' academy and the boys' grammar school are now things of the past. But in the public high school and in the college the advantages of a liberal education are offered to young men and to young women on equal terms. Thus in God's providence do the wise and good build for those who come after them.

INDEX

Arts, instruction in, 24-26, 34
Boarding schools, disadvantages of, 10-24, 28-29
Children, instruction of, 30-31
Colleges, women's, 39
Dancing, 24-25
Davis, Henry, 40, 44
Defects in female education, 9-14, 28-29
Domestic instruction, 22-24
Education, female. *See also* Instruction, female
    advantages of, 28-37
    defects in, 9-14, 28-29
    goals of, 14-18, 34-37
    improvement of, 7-8
Female Academy at Middlebury, 39-41
Family. *See also* Mothers, importance of
    female role in, 22-24
Goals of female education, 14-18, 34-37
Government
    female education as responsibility of, 18-19, 36-37, 44-45
    females as preservers of stability in, 31-34
Hart, Emma. *See* Willard, Emma Hart
Housewifery, 22-24, 35
Instruction, female
    poor quality of, 12-14
    regulations affecting, 26-28
    suitable subjects for, 20-26
Linsley, Mrs. Charles, 42
Literature, 20-21, 34
Middlebury, Vt.
    Emma Willard's life in, 39-45
Middlebury College, 43
Model for female seminary, 19-28
Morality
    females as influence on, 20, 32-34, 35
Mothers, importance of, 8, 18, 21, 22-23
Music, 25-26
Reform, necessity of, 7-8
Religion, 20, 34
Science, 21-22
Seymour, Horatio, 40
Wealth, influence of on society, 32-34
Willard, Emma Hart
    opens boarding school for girls, 42-44
    influences on, 39-41
    devises "plan for improving female education," 44
Willard, John
    encourages achievements of wife, 41-42